# BEST OF LEON RUSSELL

## Contents

- 3   The Ballad of Mad Dogs and Englishmen
- 8   Delta Lady
- 11   Girl from the North Country
- 16   Hummingbird
- 20   Lady Blue
- 27   Of Thee I Sing
- 34   Roll Away the Stone
- 42   A Song for You
- 48   Stranger in a Strange Land
- 54   Superstar
- 56   This Masquerade
- 62   Tight Rope

This book was approved by Leon Russell

Piano/vocal transcriptions by David Pearl and John Nicholas

Cherry Lane Music Company
Director of Publications/Project Editor: Mark Phillips
Manager of Publications: Gabrielle Fastman

ISBN-13: 978-1-57560-940-9
ISBN-10: 1-57560-940-1

Copyright © 2007 Cherry Lane Music Company
International Copyright Secured     All Rights Reserved

The music, text, design and graphics in this publication are protected by copyright law. Any duplication or transmission, by any means, electronic, mechanical, photocopying, recording or otherwise, is an infringement of copyright.

Visit our website at www.cherrylane.com

# LEON RUSSELL

Leon Russell played on, arranged, wrote, and/or produced some of rock-and-roll's most successful and important records. Russell reached the top of the country charts, had two Top 40 singles as a solo artist, released four gold albums, and had a hand in hundreds of other chart hits. He is, as one reviewer said, "pop music's most anonymous big shot."

Born in 1942, Russell began as an underage piano player in Oklahoma, backing such legends as Jerry Lee Lewis and Ronnie Hawkins. After Russell relocated to Los Angeles, he became part of an elite group of studio musicians called the Wrecking Crew, playing sessions for Bob Dylan, Frank Sinatra, Ike & Tina Turner, the Rolling Stones, the Byrds, the Ventures, Bobby Darin, and Herb Alpert, among others. His distinctive piano playing can be heard on Jan & Dean's "Surf City," Bobby "Boris" Pickett's "Monster Mash," and the Beach Boys' "California Girls," and many others too numerous to mention.

During his first U.S. tour, Elton John opened concerts for Leon Russell before rising to stardom himself. Elton was heard saying on a recent *Biography* special that he knew he had made it in rock-and-roll when he received a telegram from Russell congratulating him on his first hit record. Elton has credited Russell for being a huge inspiration to him during those years.

As a writer, Russell's songs have hit the charts across all genres and have been covered by a diverse range of artists. Russell was instrumental in contributing to Joe Cocker's career by organizing and leading the band on the Mad Dogs and Englishmen tour as well as writing Cocker's hit song "Delta Lady." Russell's legendary hit "This Masquerade" was the first song in music history to occupy the number one spot on the jazz, pop, and R&B charts, and George Benson's cover of the song won the Record of the Year Grammy in 1976. The Carpenters hit gold with their recording of Russell's "Superstar." Russell's "A Song for You" brought Ray Charles renown, and B.B. King had the same with Russell's "Hummingbird."

After receiving his fourth gold album for *Will o' the Wisp*, which included the hit single "Lady Blue," Russell returned to his country roots. Under the name Hank Wilson, he released a country music album, *Hank Wilson's Back*, and in 1979 he teamed with Willie Nelson and achieved success with *One for the Road*, which was honored by the Country Music Association as Album of the Year. Russell's "Heartbreak Hotel" topped the country charts, and Russell and Nelson have toured together several times since. In 1984 Russell released *Hank Wilson Vol. II*. Continuing into the 1990's, he released *Anything Can Happen*, followed by 1998's *Legend in My Time: Hank Wilson Vol. III* and 1999's *Face in the Crowd*. In 2001 Russell won a Grammy for the Earl Scruggs and Friends video *Foggy Mountain Breakdown*.

In the past several years Russell's own label, Leon Russell Records, released numerous titles from Russell: *Signature Songs*, a collection of acoustic piano/vocal recordings of Russell Classics; *Guitar Blues*, an album which was previously available only in Japan; *Moonlight & Love Songs*, a collection of standards, and the re-release of *Face in the Crowd* and *A Mighty Flood*. Also released were CDs from Connye Florance, Black Entertainment Television's (BET) Jazz Vocalist of the Year in 2000, and Mike Gallaher (Blue Paradise), jazz and touring guitarist from the Joe Cocker Band.

In 2004, Russell was notified that his "Stranger in a Strange Land" was handpicked by Mel Gibson and team for the CD *Songs Inspired by The Passion of the Christ*. In October 2006 Russell took his place among other notables as he was inducted in the Oklahoma Music Hall of Fame. And in November 2006, Russell released his latest effort, *Angel in Disguise*. Russell himself called this his "best record in 25 years."

Today, Russell's musical style is still resonating with his lifelong fans and inspiring a new crop of loyal followers of all ages.

# The Ballad of Mad Dogs and Englishmen

Words and Music by
Leon Russell

Slowly

*with pedal*

Kids and planes and run-way strikes, flash-y pimps and fam-'ly fights, spot-ted dogs and blood-shot eyes, our space cap-tain laughs and tries

---

Copyright © 1971; Renewed 1999 Dimensional Songs Of The Knoll (BMI) and Embassy Music Corporation (BMI)
Worldwide Rights for Dimensional Songs Of The Knoll Administered by Cherry River Music Co.
International Copyright Secured  All Rights Reserved

to un-der-stand the scheme of things.

And just in time the scene has changed. The bus is here;

bring the beer. Sher-man's read-ing Shake-speare.

Mov-ie mak-ers, boob-y shak-ers, and sex-y air-plane ticket tak - ers, un - ion mem - bers, Le - o Fen - der's pride and joy,

e - lec - tric toy. Teach - ers and learn - ers

and in - cense burn - ers, re - li - gious lead - ers and chron - ic bleed - ers,

thieves and pi - rates on a ride; it's a hip - pie com - mune, bo - na fide. My life and time, the war death dealers, rock-pop cor-res-pon-dence feel-ers. But O-kies and Lim-eys, cur-tain climb-ers, Stones and fu-ture Dom-i-noes, I know which way the wind blows, sto-len co-la no one knows, *(Spoken:)* "the Shadow do," but it's still a

B♭9 Am7 F F♯o7 C/G A7♯5
5fr
shad - y crew. 'Cause I love her and she loves you.
F F♯o7 C/G A7
3
Just my - self and for - ty friends in the name of Cock - er Pow - er
F F♯o7 C/G Gm/B♭ A7♯5 Dm7 G7 C
out here on the road a - gain with mad dogs and Eng - lish - men.
N.C. C7
8va
freely

# Delta Lady

Words and Music by
Leon Russell

| Em/B | C/B♭ |

whis - per sighs to sat - is - fy your long - ing
think of days and dif-f'rent ways I've held you.
yet it seems the cit - y scene is lack - ing.

| F/A  F | C | G7 | C |

for the warm and ten - der shel - ter of my bod - y.
We were close - ly touch - ing, yes our heart was beat - ing. } Oh, you're
I'm so glad you're wait - ing for me in the coun - try.

| C/B♭ | F | C | *To Coda* ⊕ |

mine, yes, you're mine, Del - ta La - dy. Yes, you're

| C/B♭ | F | C  C/E  F | 1.  G9♯5 |
                           N.C.

mine, be all mine, Del - ta La - dy.

9

2.
C/G G9♯5 Dm G7/B Dm
Oh, when I'm home again in England,
mp
B♭ F
I'll think of you, love.
Because I
cresc.
D.S. al Coda
C C/E F N.C. C/G C C/E F N.C. G9♯5
love you, love.
mf
Coda
C/B♭ F C
Repeat and fade
mine, be all mine, Delta Lady. Yes, you're
mine, yes, you're mine, Delta Lady. Yes, you're

# Girl from the North Country

*Words and Music by Bob Dylan*

**Moderately**

If you're trav-'lin' to the north coun-try fair, where the winds hit heav-y on the bor-der line,

Copyright © 1963 (Renewed) Special Rider Music (ASCAP)
International Copyright Secured   All Rights Reserved

11

re-mem-ber me to the one who lives there.

She once was a true love of mine.

Oh, please

see her hair's hang-in' long, it flows and rolls all down her breast. Please see for me if her hair is hang-in' long. Oh, that is the way I re-member her best. If you go when the snow flakes fall, when the riv-

(Lyrics)

...ers freeze and the summer ends, see for me she has a coat so warm to keep her from the howling winds.

So if you're trav-'lin' in the north country

fair, _____ where the winds hit heav-y on the bor-der-line, _____ re-mem-ber me _____ to one _____ who lives _____ there. _____ She once _____ was _____ a true _____ love, true love _____ of _____ mine. Ooh.

# Hummingbird

Words and Music by
Leon Russell

| Bb | | A | |
|---|---|---|---|

—— way. ———— hum - ming - bird. And have you heard
And I just have to say, that I in my

| Dm | | Bb | |
|---|---|---|---|

thought —— my —— life had end - ed? But I
life —— I —— love no oth - er, be - cause she's

| Dm | | G7 | |
|---|---|---|---|

find —— that it's just be - gun, 'cause } And } she
more —— than I de - serve.

| Dm | | Eb9b5 | |
|---|---|---|---|

gets me where I live. I'll give all I have to give. I'm

17

talking about that hummingbird. ___ Oh, she's
little and she loves me, ___ too ___ much for words to say. ___ When I
see her in the mornings ___ sleeping, ___ she's
little and she loves me to ___ my lucky days. Humming-

1.
F/G
B♭/C
C
A+
A7
bird, don't fly a - way.
N.C.
2.
B♭
A
B♭/C
C
B♭
When I'm way. Don't fly a - way,
F
C
Repeat and fade
a - way. Don't fly a -

# Lady Blue

Words and Music by
Leon Russell

Well, you're show-ing me a dif-f'rent side, e-ven

C/D
Dm
Am
asked if the flame has died. You're get - tin'
B♭maj7
Am
Gm7
3fr
used to me, ba - by. But
Asus4
A
Dm
you just wait and see, la - dy,
B♭maj7
Am7
Gm7
3fr
'cause I've been in love be - fore,

and I love you a whole lot more. _____ And if you want it to be ____ real ____ good to you ____ when I'm ____ lay- in' ____ here mak- in' love ____ to you, lis- ten real close to me, ____ la - dy. I wan - na get it straight right ____ now, ____ oh, ____ baby, 'cause I \_\_\_\_\_ love you more and more and more, \_\_\_\_\_ Lady Blue.

Sad baby, blue lady, sing \_\_\_\_\_ me a love \_\_\_\_\_ song. I just \_\_\_\_\_ want you to know \_\_\_\_\_

that I \_\_\_ love you more \_\_\_ and more and more and more. \_\_\_

So if you

Fmaj9
3fr
C/D
Dm
want it to be real good to you when I'm lay-in' here mak-in' love
Am
B♭maj7
Am
Gm7
3fr
to you, lis-ten real close to me, ba - by.
Asus4
A
You just wait and see,
Dm
B♭maj7
Am7
Gm7
3fr
la - dy. I got-ta whole lot-ta love

Asus4
to give ya. I got-ta whole life to spend if you'll
A
Bbmaj7
Am
Gm7
Bb/C
just let me sing sweet love songs, La-dy
Fmaj9
Bb/C
Fmaj9
Blue. Oh, sing a love song,
Bb/C
Fmaj9
Bb/C
Fmaj9
La-dy Blue.

# Of Thee I Sing

Words and Music by
Leon Russell

G7
I don't know ex - act - ly just what's
And the bud is on the books in
C7
Eb9
D7
go - in' down.
O - hi - o.
I guess I'll hang a - round un - til I
It's so bad and strange. What can I
G7
C
G
see.
say?
Woh, she's pret - ty like a knife. She
C
G
Fsus2
C
cuts in e - ven more; she chang - es right be - fore my eyes in - to some - thin'

ug - ly and sore. You do pret - ty like a knife. She cuts in e - ven more; she chang - es right be - fore my eyes in - to some - thin' strange, and more.

Woh, _____ she's

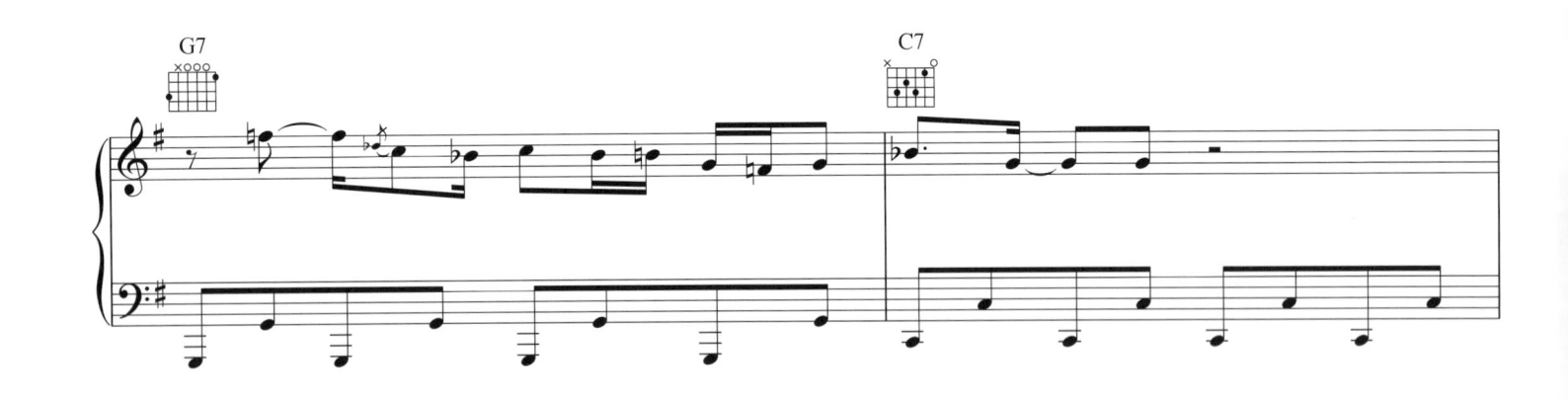

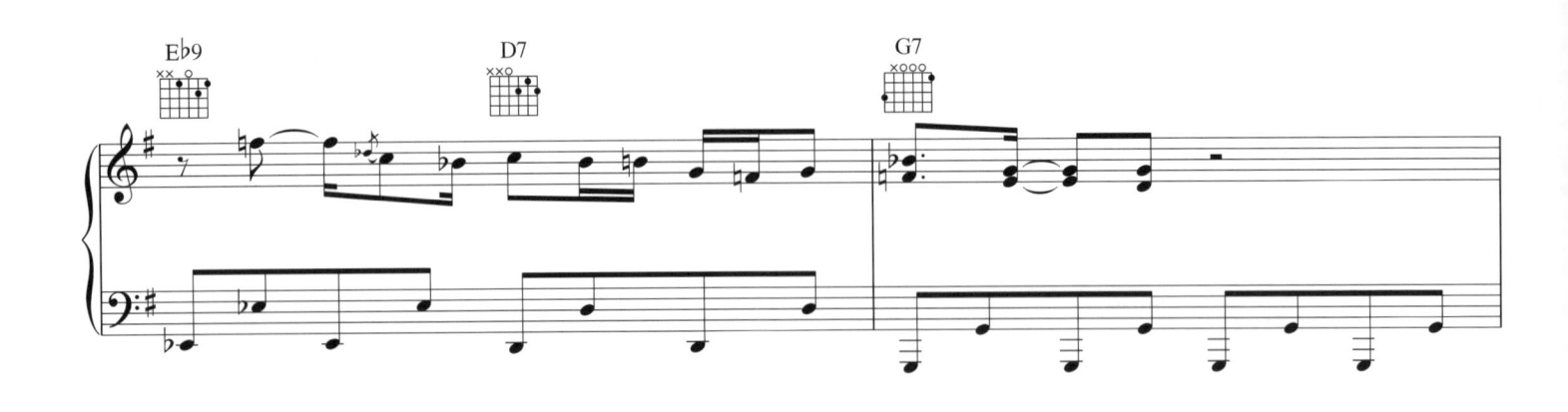

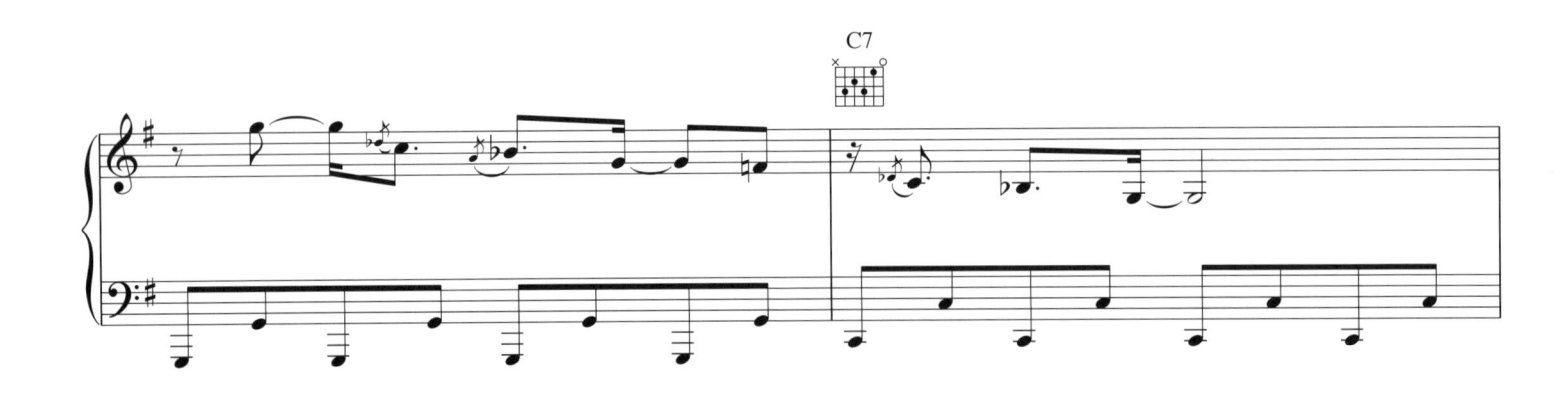

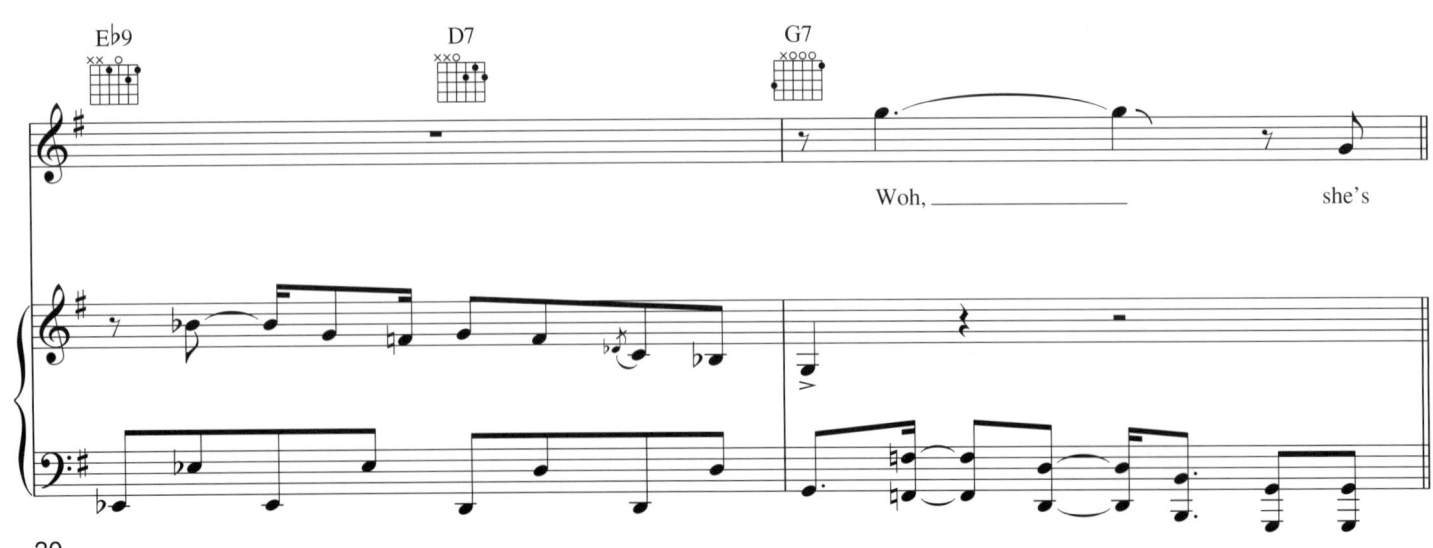

pret - ty like a knife. She cuts in e - ven more; she chang - es

right be - fore my eyes in - to some - thin' ug - ly and sore. You do

pret - ty like a knife. She cuts in e - ven more; she chang - es

right be - fore my eyes in - to some - thin' strange,

32

33

# Roll Away the Stone

Words and Music by
Leon Russell and Greg Dempsey

Well, it's such a

Dm
Eb7
E7
F7
strange world that I'm livin' in.
She was my woman and he
8va
Bb7
A7
N.C.
was my friend, but I was wrong again.
Such
Dm
Eb7
E7
F7
strange changes that you put me through,
but like a fool I'm still in
Bb7
A7
Bb7
love with you. What can this poor boy do?
Roll away the stone.

F7
B♭7
F7
Don't leave me here a - lone.
Res - ur - rect
C
B♭
A
me and pro - tect me.
Don't leave me lay - in' here.
Dm
G
B♭/C
Am/C
B♭/F
F
What will they do in two thous - and years?
Dm
G
Dm
8va

G
N.C.
Dm
E♭7
E7
It's such a strange time that we're passin' through.
F7
B♭7
Asus4
A7
I thought you'd tell me when your time was due. I guess you thought I knew.
N.C.
Dm
E♭7
E7
Oh, strange way to keep from hurt-ing me.
F7
B♭7
A7
Why did you lie? How could I help but be? Oh, won't you help me, please?
8va
gliss.

Roll a-way the stone. Don't leave me here a-lone. Res-ur-rect me and pro-tect me. Don't leave me lay-in' here. What will they do in two thous-and years? Roll a-way the stone.

F7
B♭7
F7
Don't leave me here a - lone.
Roll a - way,
B♭7
F7
B♭7
roll a - way the stone.
Roll a - way the stone.
F7
B♭7
F7
Roll a - way, roll a - way, roll a - way the stone.
Roll

B♭7
F7
a - way the stone.
Roll a - way,
roll a - way the stone.
F7
B♭7
Roll a - way the stone.
F7
B♭7
F
N.C.
Roll a - way, roll a - way the stone.
3
mp
3
3
rit.
F7
8va
gliss.
Ped.
*

# A Song for You

*Words and Music by Leon Russell*

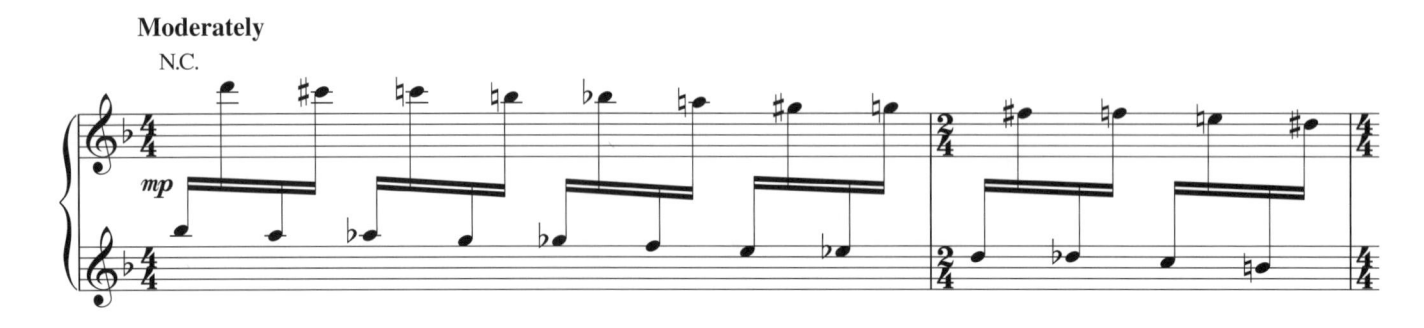

I've been so many places in my life and time.

I've sung a lot of songs; I've made some bad rhyme. I've

acted out my love in stag - es with ten thou-sand peo-ple watch-ing.

But we're a-lone now and I'm sing-ing this song to you.

I know your im-age of me is what I hope to be.

I treat-ed you un-kind-ly but, dar-ling, can't you see there's no one more im-por-tant to ___ me? Dar - ling, can't you please see through ___ me,

'cause we're a - lone now and I'm sing - ing this song to you. ___ You

taught me pre - cious se - crets of the truth, ___ with - hold - ing noth - ing.

You came out in front ___ and I ___ was hid - ing. ___

| Dm | F+/C# | F6/C | Bm7♭5 |

But now I'm so much bet - ter. And if my words don't come to - geth - er,

| B♭ | F6/A | G7 | C7sus4 | C7 |

lis - ten to the mel - o - dy 'cause my love's in there hid - ing.

N.C.

𝄋 Dm | C#°

I love you in a place where there's no space or time.

Play 1st time only
F/C
Bm7♭5
I love you, for in my life you are a friend of mine.
Play 2nd time only
Bm7♭5
G7/B
B♭
Am7
of mine.
And when my life is o - ver, re -
Gm7
3fr
Am7
B♭
Am/C
To Coda
mem - ber when we were to - geth - er.
We were a - lone and I was sing - ing
B♭/C
F
E♭
Dm/E♭
E♭
N.C.
this song to you.
mf
mp

this song for you. We were a-lone and I was sing-ing this song for you. We were a-lone and I was sing-ing my song, sing-ing this song for you.

# Stranger in a Strange Land

Words and Music by
Leon Russell and Don J. Preston

*Moderately slow*

How many days has it been since I was born? How many days until I die? Do I know any ways that

How many miles will it take to see the sun? And how many years until it's done? Kiss my confusion a-

Copyright © 1971 IRVING MUSIC, INC.
Copyright Renewed
All Rights Reserved   Used by Permission

48

I can make you laugh, or do I only know how to make you
way in the night. Lay by my side when the morn-ing
cry? When the ba-by looks a-round him, it's such a sight to see. He
comes. And the ba-by looks a-round him and shares his bed of hay with the
shares a sim-ple sec-ret with the wise man. He's a stran-
bur-row in the pal-ace of the king.
ger in a strange land. Just a stran-

ger in a strange land. Tell me why he's a stranger in a strange land. Just a stranger in a strange land.

(Lyrics)

Well, I don't exactly know what's goin' on in the world today. Don't know what there is to say about the way the people are treating each other. Not like brothers. Leaders take us far away from ecology with mythology and astrology. Has got some words to say about the way we live today. Why can't we learn to love each other? It's time to learn a new faith to the whole world-wide human race

and stop the money chase and lay back, relax, and get back on the human track.

And stop racing toward oblivion. Oh, such a sad, sad state we're in. And

that's a thing. Do you recognize the bells of truth when you hear them ring? Won't you stop and listen to the chil - dren sing? _ Oh, won't you sing it, chil - dren? Won't you come on and sing it, chil - dren? _

(Stran - ger in _ a strange _ land.) _ Woh, _ sing it one more time. _

(Stran - ger in _ a strange _ land.) _

# Superstar

Words and Music by
Leon Russell and Bonnie Sheridan

Moderately slow

1. Long ago, and, oh, so far away, I fell in love with you before the second show. Your guitar, it sounds so sweet and clear, but you're not really here, it's just the

2. Loneliness is such a sad affair, and I can hardly wait to be with you again. What to say, to make you come again? Come back to me again, and play your

Copyright © 1970, 1971; Renewed 1998, 1999 Dimensional Songs Of The Knoll (BMI), Embassy Music Corporation (BMI)
and Delbon Publishing Company, Inc. (BMI)
Worldwide Rights for Dimensional Songs Of The Knoll Administered by Cherry River Music Co.
International Copyright Secured   All Rights Reserved

**Chorus**

ra - di - o.
sad gui - tar.
Don't you re-mem-ber you told me you love me, ba-by? You said you'd be com-ing back this way a-gain may-be. Ba-by, ba-by, ba-by, ba-by, oh, ba-by, I love you,

1.
I real-ly do.

2.
I real-ly do.

# This Masquerade

Words and Music by
Leon Russell

Moderately slow

Are we really happy here with this lonely game we play, looking for words to say?

Copyright © 1972, 1973; Renewed 2000, 2001 Dimensional Songs Of The Knoll (BMI) and Embassy Music Corporation (BMI)
Worldwide Rights for Dimensional Songs Of The Knoll Administered by Cherry River Music Co.
International Copyright Secured   All Rights Reserved

Search-ing but not find-ing un-der-stand-ing an-y way,\_\_\_ we're lost in a mas-quer-ade.\_\_\_ Both a-fraid to say\_\_ we're just\_\_ too far\_\_ a-way\_\_ from be-ing close to-geth-

Ab7-9
Dbmaj7
-er from the start.
We
Dm7
G7
G7+5
Cmaj9
tried to talk it o - ver, but the words got in the way.
Gm7
G6
G+
C7
Gm7
We're lost in - side this lone - ly game we play.
C9
Gb13+11
Fm
Fm(+7)
Thoughts of leav - ing dis - ap - pear ev' - ry
mp

| Fm7 | Bb9 | Fm |

time I see your eyes ____ No mat-ter how hard ____

| Db7 | Gm7 | C7-9 |

I try ____

| Fm | Fm(+7) | Fm7 |

to un-der-stand the rea-sons that we car-ry on ____ this way, ____

| Bb9 | Db9 | C7 *To Coda* |

____ we're lost ____ in this mas - quer-ade. ____

*Guitar solo sounds 8va lower than written.

quer - ade.

# Tight Rope

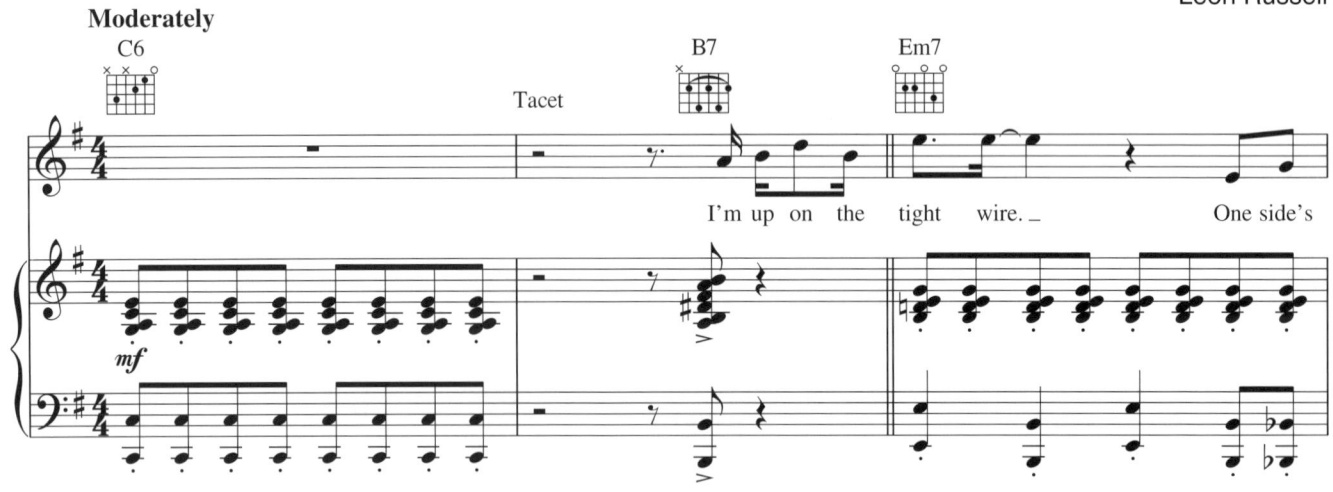

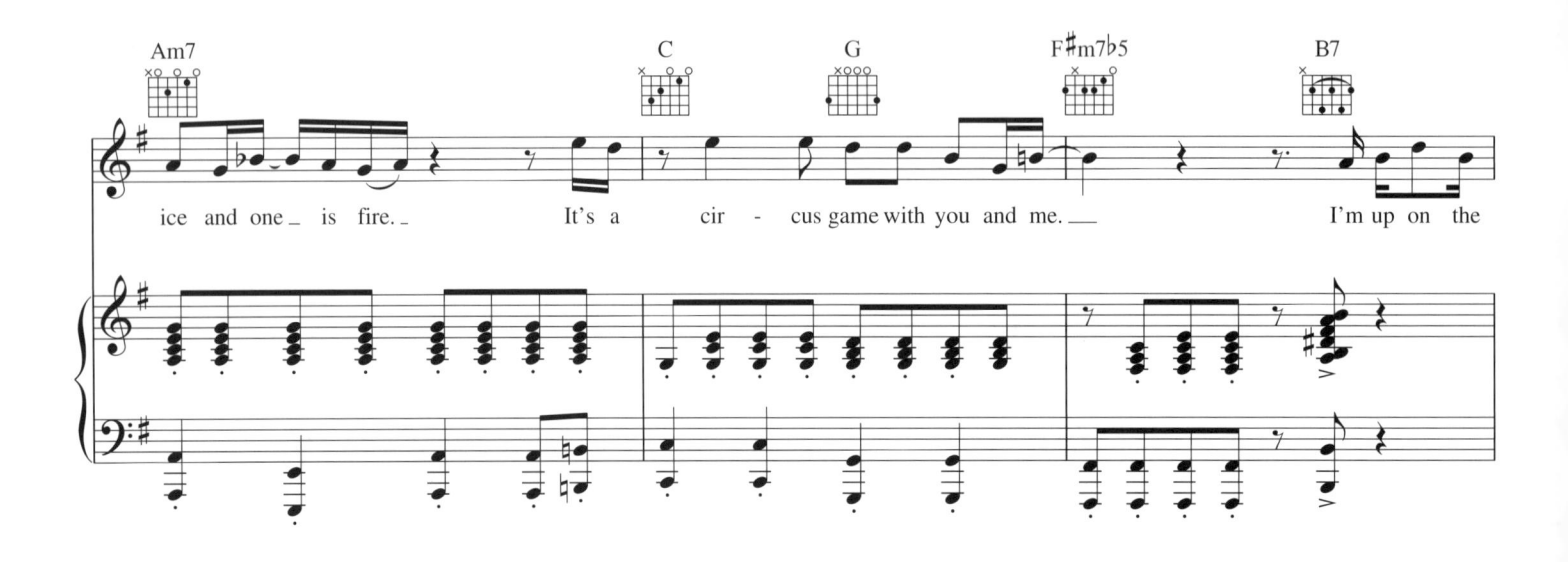

Words and Music by
Leon Russell

Moderately

I'm up on the tight wire. One side's ice and one is fire. It's a circus game with you and me. I'm up on the tight-rope. One side's hate and one is hope. But the top-hat on my head is all you see.

Copyright © 1972 IRVING MUSIC, INC.
Copyright Renewed
All Rights Reserved   Used by Permission

And the wire seems to be the on-ly place for me. A com-e-dy of er-rors and I'm fall-ing. Like a rub-ber neck gi-raffe, you look in-to my past. Well, ba-by, you're just too blind to see I'm up in the spot-light. Oh, does it feel right. Oh, the al-ti-tude seems to get to me.

I'm up on the tight wire, \_\_\_ flanked by life and the fu-n'ral pyre, \_\_\_ put-ting on \_\_ a show \_\_ for you \_\_ to see. \_\_\_

Like a

C
G
F♯m7♭5
B7
Em7
Am7
C
G
F♯m7♭5
B7
Em7
Am7
C
G
8va
gliss.
Begin fade
F♯m7♭5
B7
Em7
Am7
Fade out

# great songs series

Cherry Lane Music is proud to present this legendary series which has delighted players and performers for generations.

### Great Songs of the Fifties

The latest release in Cherry Lane's acclaimed Great Songs series, this songbook presents 51 musical memories from the fabulous '50s! Features rock, pop, country, Broadway and movie tunes, including: All Shook Up • At the Hop • Blue Suede Shoes • Dream Lover • Fly Me to the Moon • Kansas City • Love Me Tender • Misty • Peggy Sue • Rock Around the Clock • Sea of Love • Sixteen Tons • Take the "A" Train • Wonderful! Wonderful! • and more. Includes an introduction by award-winning journalist Bruce Pollock.

_____02500323 P/V/G..............................$16.95

### Great Songs of the Sixties, Vol. 1 – Revised Edition

The newly updated version of this classic book includes 80 faves from the 1960s: Angel of the Morning • Bridge over Troubled Water • Cabaret • Different Drum • Do You Believe in Magic • Eve of Destruction • Georgy Girl • It Was a Very Good Year • Monday, Monday • People • Spinning Wheel • Walk on By • and more.

_____02509902 P/V/G..............................$19.95

### Great Songs of the Sixties, Vol. 2 – Revised Edition

61 more 60s hits: And When I Die • California Dreamin' • Crying • The 59th Street Bridge Song (Feelin' Groovy) • For Once in My Life • Honey • Little Green Apples • MacArthur Park • Me and Bobby McGee • Nowhere Man • Piece of My Heart • Sugar, Sugar • You Made Me So Very Happy • and more.

_____02509904 P/V/G..............................$19.95

### Great Songs of the Seventies – Revised Edition

This super collection of 70 big hits from the '70s includes: After the Love Has Gone • Afternoon Delight • Annie's Song • Band on the Run • Cold as Ice • FM • Imagine • It's Too Late • Layla • Let It Be • Maggie May • Piano Man • Shelter from the Storm • Superstar • Sweet Baby James • Time in a Bottle • The Way We Were • more!

_____02509917 P/V/G..............................$19.95

*Prices, contents, and availability subject to change without notice.*

### Great Songs of the Seventies – Volume 2

Features 58 outstanding '70s songs in rock, pop, country, Broadway and movie genres: American Woman • Baby, I'm-A Want You • Day by Day • Do That to Me One More Time • Dog & Butterfly • Don't Cry Out Loud • Dreamboat Annie • Follow Me • Get Closer • Grease • Heard It in a Love Song • I'll Be There • It's a Heartache • The Loco-Motion • My Eyes Adored You • New Kid in Town • Night Fever • On and On • Sing • Summer Breeze • Tonight's the Night • We Are the Champions • Y.M.C.A. • and more. Includes articles by Cherry Lane Music Company founder Milt Okun, and award-winning music journalist Bruce Pollock.

_____02500322 P/V/G..............................$19.95

### Great Songs of the Eighties – Revised Edition

This newly revised edition features 50 songs in rock, pop & country styles, plus hits from Broadway and the movies! Songs: Almost Paradise • Angel of the Morning • Do You Really Want to Hurt Me • Endless Love • Flashdance...What a Feeling • Guilty • Hungry Eyes • (Just Like) Starting Over • Let Love Rule • Missing You • Patience • Through the Years • Time After Time • Total Eclipse of the Heart • and more.

_____02502125 P/V/G..............................$18.95

### Great Songs of the Nineties

This terrific collection features 48 big hits in many styles. Includes: Achy Breaky Heart • Beautiful in My Eyes • Believe • Black Hole Sun • Black Velvet • Blaze of Glory • Building a Mystery • Crash into Me • Fields of Gold • From a Distance • Glycerine • Here and Now • Hold My Hand • I'll Make Love to You • Ironic • Linger • My Heart Will Go On • Waterfalls • Wonderwall • and more.

_____02500040 P/V/G..............................$16.95

### Great Songs of the Pop Era

Over 50 hits from the pop era, including: Amazed • Annie's Song • Ebony and Ivory • Every Breath You Take • Hey Nineteen • I Want to Know What Love Is • I'm Every Woman • Just the Two of Us • Leaving on a Jet Plane • My Cherie Amour • Raindrops Keep Fallin' on My Head • Rocky Mountain High • This Is the Moment • Time After Time • (I've Had) the Time of My Life • What a Wonderful World • and more!

_____02500043 Easy Piano.....................$16.95

**CHERRY LANE MUSIC COMPANY**
6 East 32nd Street, New York, NY 10016

*Quality in Printed Music*

Visit Cherry Lane on the Internet at
**www.cherrylane.com**

Exclusively Distributed By
**HAL•LEONARD® CORPORATION**
7777 W. Bluemound Rd. P.O. Box 13819 Milwaukee, WI 53213

0402

# More Big-Note & Easy Piano Books

For a complete listing of Cherry Lane titles available, including contents listings, please visit our web site at www.cherrylane.com

### CLASSICAL CHRISTMAS
Easy solo arrangements of 30 wonderful holiday songs: Ave Maria • Dance of the Sugar Plum Fairy • Evening Prayer • Gesu Bambino • Hallelujah! • He Shall Feed His Flock • March of the Toys • O Come, All Ye Faithful • O Holy Night • Pastoral Symphony • Sheep May Safely Graze • Sinfonia • Waltz of the Flowers • and more.
___02500112 Easy Piano Solo ......$9.95

### BEST OF JOHN DENVER
___02505512 Easy Piano .............$9.95

### DOWN THE AISLE
Easy piano arrangements of 20 beloved pop and classical wedding songs, including: Air on the G String • Ave Maria • Canon in D • Follow Me • Give Me Forever (I Do) • Jesu, Joy of Man's Desiring • Prince of Denmark's March • Through the Years • Trumpet Tune • Unchained Melody • Wedding March • When I Fall in Love • You Decorated My Life • and more.
___025000267 Easy Piano ............$9.95

### EASY BROADWAY SHOWSTOPPERS
Easy piano arrangements of 16 traditional and new Broadway standards, including: "Impossible Dream" from *Man of La Mancha* • "Unusual Way" from *Nine* • "This Is the Moment" from *Jekyll & Hyde* • many more.
___02505517 Easy Piano ...........$12.95

### GOLD AND GLORY – THE ROAD TO EL DORADO
This beautiful souvenir songbook features full-color photos and 8 songs from the DreamWorks animated film. Includes original songs by Elton John and Tim Rice, and a score by Hans Zimmer and John Powell. Songs: Cheldorado – Score • El Dorado • Friends Never Say Goodbye • It's Tough to Be a God • Someday out of the Blue (Theme from El Dorado) • The Trail We Blaze • Without Question • Wonders of the New World: To Shibalba.
___02500274 Easy Piano ............$14.95

### A FAMILY CHRISTMAS AROUND THE PIANO
25 songs for hours of family fun, including: Away in a Manger • Deck the Hall • The First Noel • God Rest Ye Merry, Gentlemen • Hark! the Herald Angels Sing • Jingle Bells • Jolly Old St. Nicholas • Joy to the World • O Little Town of Bethlehem • Silent Night, Holy Night • The Twelve Days of Christmas • and more.
___02500398 Easy Piano ..............$7.95

### GILBERT & SULLIVAN FOR EASY PIANO
20 great songs from 6 great shows by this beloved duo renowned for their comedic classics. Includes: Behold the Lord High Executioner • The Flowers That Bloom in the Spring • He Is an Englishman • I Am the Captain of the Pinafore • (I'm Called) Little Buttercup • Miya Sama • Three Little Maids • Tit-Willow • We Sail the Ocean Blue • When a Merry Maiden Marries • When Britain Really Ruled the Waves • When Frederic Was a Lad • and more.
___02500270 Easy Piano ............$12.95

### GREAT CONTEMPORARY BALLADS
___02500150 Easy Piano ............$12.95

### HOLY CHRISTMAS CAROLS COLORING BOOK
A terrific songbook with 7 sacred carols and lots of coloring pages for the young pianist. Songs include: Angels We Have Heard on High • The First Noel • Hark! The Herald Angels Sing • It Came upon a Midnight Clear • O Come All Ye Faithful • O Little Town of Bethlehem • Silent Night.
___02500277 Five-Finger Piano ....$6.95

### JEKYLL & HYDE – VOCAL SELECTIONS
Ten songs from the Wildhorn/Bricusse Broadway smash, arranged for big-note: In His Eyes • It's a Dangerous Game • Lost in the Darkness • A New Life • No One Knows Who I Am • Once Upon a Dream • Someone Like You • Sympathy, Tenderness • Take Me as I Am • This Is the Moment.
___02505515 Easy Piano ............$12.95
___02500023 Big-Note Piano ........$9.95

### JUST FOR KIDS – *NOT!* CHRISTMAS SONGS
This unique collection of 14 Christmas favorites is fun for the whole family! Kids can play the full-sounding big-note solos alone, or with their parents (or teachers) playing accompaniment for the thrill of four-hand piano! Includes: Deck the Halls • Jingle Bells • Silent Night • What Child Is This? • and more.
___02505510 Big-Note Piano ........$7.95

### JUST FOR KIDS – *NOT!* CLASSICS
Features big-note arrangements of classical masterpieces, plus optional accompaniment for adults. Songs: Air on the G String • Dance of the Sugar Plum Fairy • Für Elise • Jesu, Joy of Man's Desiring • Ode to Joy • Pomp and Circumstance • The Sorcerer's Apprentice • William Tell Overture • and more!
___02505513 Classics....................$7.95
___02500301 More Classics ..........$7.95

### JUST FOR KIDS – *NOT!* FUN SONGS
Fun favorites for kids everywhere in big-note arrangements for piano, including: Bingo • Eensy Weensy Spider • Farmer in the Dell • Jingle Bells • London Bridge • Pop Goes the Weasel • Puff the Magic Dragon • Skip to My Lou • Twinkle, Twinkle Little Star • and more!
___02505523 Fun Songs................$7.95
___02505528 More Fun Songs ......$7.95

### JUST FOR KIDS – *NOT!* TV THEMES & MOVIE SONGS
Entice the kids to the piano with this delightful collection of songs and themes from movies and TV. These big-note arrangements include themes from The Brady Bunch and The Addams Family, as well as Do-Re-Mi (The Sound of Music), theme from Beetlejuice (Day-O) and Puff the Magic Dragon. Each song includes an accompaniment part for teacher or adult so that the kids can experience the joy of four-hand playing as well! Plus performance tips.
___02505507 TV Themes & Movie Songs .......................$9.95
___02500304 More TV Themes & Movie Songs .......................$9.95

### LOVE BALLADS
___02500152 EZ-Play Today #364 $7.95

### MERRY CHRISTMAS, EVERYONE
Over 20 contemporary and classic all-time holiday favorites arranged for big-note piano or easy piano. Includes: Away in a Manger • Christmas Like a Lullaby • The First Noel • Joy to the World • The Marvelous Toy • and more.
___02505600 Big-Note Piano ........$9.95

See your local music dealer or contact:

**CHERRY LANE MUSIC COMPANY**
6 East 32nd Street, New York, NY 10016

EXCLUSIVELY DISTRIBUTED BY

**HAL•LEONARD**
7777 W. BLUEMOUND RD. P.O. BOX 13819 MILWAUKEE, WI 53213

### POKEMON 2 B.A. MASTER
This great songbook features easy piano arrangements of 13 tunes from the hit TV series: 2.B.A. Master • Double Trouble (Team Rocket) • Everything Changes • Misty's Song • My Best Friends • Pokémon (Dance Mix) • Pokémon Theme • PokéRAP • The Time Has Come (Pikachu's Goodbye) • Together, Forever • Viridian City • What Kind of Pokémon Are You? • You Can Do It (If You Really Try). Includes a full-color, 8-page pull-out section featuring characters and scenes from this super hot show.
___02500145 Easy Piano ............$12.95

### POKEMON
Five-finger arrangements of 7 songs from the hottest show for kids! Includes: Pokémon Theme • The Time Has Come (Pikachu's Goodbye) • 2B A Master • Together, Forever • What Kind of Pokémon Are You? • You Can Do It (If You Really Try). Also features cool character artwork, and a special section listing the complete lyrics for the "PokéRAP."
___02500291 Five-Finger Piano ....$7.95

### POP/ROCK HITS
___02500153 E-Z Play Today #366 $7.95

### POP/ROCK LOVE SONGS
Easy arrangements of 18 romatic favorites, including: Always • Bed of Roses • Butterfly Kisses • Follow Me • From This Moment On • Hard Habit to Break • Leaving on a Jet Plane • When You Say Nothing at All • more.
___02500151 Easy Piano ............$10.95

### POPULAR CHRISTMAS CAROLS COLORING BOOK
Kids are sure to love this fun holiday songbook! It features five-finger piano arrangements of seven Christmas classics, complete with coloring pages throughout! Songs include: Deck the Hall • Good King Wenceslas • Jingle Bells • Jolly Old St. Nicholas • O Christmas Tree • Up on the Housetop • We Wish You a Merry Christmas.
___02500276 Five-Finger Piano ....$6.95

### PUFF THE MAGIC DRAGON & 54 OTHER ALL-TIME CHILDREN'S FAVORITE SONGS
55 timeless songs enjoyed by generations of kids, and sure to be favorites for years to come. Songs include: A-Tisket A-Tasket • Alouette • Eensy Weensy Spider • The Farmer in the Dell • I've Been Working on the Railroad • If You're Happy and You Know It • Joy to the World • Michael Finnegan • Oh Where, Oh Where Has My Little Dog Gone • Silent Night • Skip to My Lou • This Old Man • and many more.
___02500017 Big-Note Piano ......$12.95

### PURE ROMANCE
___02500268 Easy Piano ............$10.95

### SCHOOLHOUSE ROCK SONGBOOK
10 unforgettable songs from the classic television educational series, now experiencing a booming resurgence in popularity from Generation X'ers to today's kids! Includes: I'm Just a Bill • Conjunction Junction • Lolly, Lolly, Lolly (Get Your Adverbs Here) • The Great American Melting Pot • and more.
___02505576 Big-Note Piano ........$8.95

### BEST OF JOHN TESH
___02505511 Easy Piano ............$12.95
___02500128 E-Z Play Today #356 $8.95

### TOP COUNTRY HITS
___02500154 E-Z Play Today #365 $7.95

Prices, contents, and availability subject to change without notice.

1001

# More Great Piano/Vocal Books
## FROM CHERRY LANE

For a complete listing of Cherry Lane titles available, including contents listings, please visit our web site at
**www.cherrylane.com**

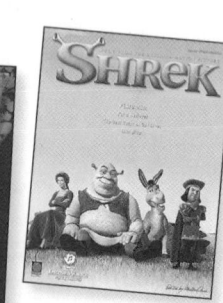

|  |  |  |
|---|---|---|
| 02500343 | Almost Famous | $14.95 |
| 02502171 | The Best of Boston | $17.95 |
| 02500672 | Black Eyed Peas – Elephunk | $17.95 |
| 02500665 | Sammy Cahn Songbook | $24.95 |
| 02500144 | Mary Chapin Carpenter – Party Doll & Other Favorites | $16.95 |
| 02502163 | Mary Chapin Carpenter – Stones in the Road | $17.95 |
| 02502165 | John Denver Anthology – Revised | $22.95 |
| 02502227 | John Denver – A Celebration of Life | $14.95 |
| 02500002 | John Denver Christmas | $14.95 |
| 02502166 | John Denver's Greatest Hits | $17.95 |
| 02502151 | John Denver – A Legacy in Song (Softcover) | $24.95 |
| 02502152 | John Denver – A Legacy in Song (Hardcover) | $34.95 |
| 02500566 | Poems, Prayers and Promises: The Art and Soul of John Denver | $19.95 |
| 02500326 | John Denver – The Wildlife Concert | $17.95 |
| 02500501 | John Denver and the Muppets: A Christmas Together | $9.95 |
| 02509922 | The Songs of Bob Dylan | $29.95 |
| 02500586 | Linda Eder – Broadway My Way | $14.95 |
| 02500497 | Linda Eder – Gold | $14.95 |
| 02500396 | Linda Eder – Christmas Stays the Same | $17.95 |
| 02500175 | Linda Eder – It's No Secret Anymore | $14.95 |
| 02502209 | Linda Eder – It's Time | $17.95 |
| 02500630 | Donald Fagen – 5 of the Best | $7.95 |
| 02500535 | Erroll Garner Anthology | $19.95 |
| 02500270 | Gilbert & Sullivan for Easy Piano | $12.95 |
| 02500318 | Gladiator | $12.95 |
| 02500273 | Gold & Glory: The Road to El Dorado | $16.95 |
| 02502126 | Best of Guns N' Roses | $17.95 |
| 02502072 | Guns N' Roses – Selections from Use Your Illusion I and II | $17.95 |
| 02500014 | Sir Roland Hanna Collection | $19.95 |
| 02500352 | Hanson – This Time Around | $16.95 |
| 02502134 | Best of Lenny Kravitz | $12.95 |
| 02500012 | Lenny Kravitz – 5 | $16.95 |
| 02500381 | Lenny Kravitz – Greatest Hits | $14.95 |
| 02503701 | Man of La Mancha | $10.95 |
| 02500693 | Dave Matthews – Some Devil | $16.95 |
| 02500555 | Dave Matthews Band – Busted Stuff | $16.95 |
| 02500003 | Dave Matthews Band – Before These Crowded Streets | $17.95 |
| 02502199 | Dave Matthews Band – Crash | $17.95 |
| 02500390 | Dave Matthews Band – Everyday | $14.95 |
| 02500493 | Dave Matthews Band – Live in Chicago 12/19/98 at the United Center | $14.95 |
| 02502192 | Dave Matthews Band – Under the Table and Dreaming | $17.95 |
| 02500681 | John Mayer – Heavier Things | $16.95 |
| 02500563 | John Mayer – Room for Squares | $16.95 |
| 02500081 | Natalie Merchant – Ophelia | $14.95 |
| 02500423 | Natalie Merchant – Tigerlily | $14.95 |
| 02502895 | Nine | $17.95 |
| 02500425 | Time and Love: The Art and Soul of Laura Nyro | $19.95 |
| 02502204 | The Best of Metallica | $17.95 |
| 02500407 | O-Town | $14.95 |
| 02500010 | Tom Paxton – The Honor of Your Company | $17.95 |
| 02507962 | Peter, Paul & Mary – Holiday Concert | $17.95 |
| 02500145 | Pokemon 2.B.A. Master | $12.95 |
| 02500026 | The Prince of Egypt | $16.95 |
| 02500660 | Best of Bonnie Raitt | $17.95 |
| 02502189 | The Bonnie Raitt Collection | $22.95 |
| 02502230 | Bonnie Raitt – Fundamental | $17.95 |
| 02502139 | Bonnie Raitt – Longing in Their Hearts | $16.95 |
| 02502088 | Bonnie Raitt – Luck of the Draw | $14.95 |
| 02507958 | Bonnie Raitt – Nick of Time | $14.95 |
| 02502190 | Bonnie Raitt – Road Tested | $24.95 |
| 02502218 | Kenny Rogers – The Gift | $16.95 |
| 02500072 | Saving Private Ryan | $14.95 |
| 02500197 | SHeDAISY – The Whole SHeBANG | $14.95 |
| 02500414 | Shrek | $14.95 |
| 02500536 | Spirit – Stallion of the Cimarron | $16.95 |
| 02500166 | Steely Dan – Anthology | $17.95 |
| 02500622 | Steely Dan – Everything Must Go | $14.95 |
| 02500284 | Steely Dan – Two Against Nature | $14.95 |
| 02500165 | Best of Steely Dan | $14.95 |
| 02500344 | Billy Strayhorn: An American Master | $17.95 |
| 02502132 | Barbra Streisand – Back to Broadway | $19.95 |
| 02500515 | Barbra Streisand – Christmas Memories | $16.95 |
| 02507969 | Barbra Streisand – A Collection: Greatest Hits and More | $17.95 |
| 02502164 | Barbra Streisand – The Concert | $22.95 |
| 02500550 | Essential Barbra Streisand | $24.95 |
| 02502228 | Barbra Streisand – Higher Ground | $16.95 |
| 02500196 | Barbra Streisand – A Love Like Ours | $16.95 |
| 02500280 | Barbra Streisand – Timeless | $19.95 |
| 02503617 | John Tesh – Avalon | $15.95 |
| 02502178 | The John Tesh Collection | $17.95 |
| 02503623 | John Tesh – A Family Christmas | $15.95 |
| 02505511 | John Tesh – Favorites for Easy Piano | $12.95 |
| 02503630 | John Tesh – Grand Passion | $16.95 |
| 02500124 | John Tesh – One World | $14.95 |
| 02500307 | John Tesh – Pure Movies 2 | $16.95 |
| 02500565 | Thoroughly Modern Millie | $17.95 |
| 02500576 | Toto – 5 of the Best | $7.95 |
| 02502175 | Tower of Power – Silver Anniversary | $17.95 |
| 02502198 | The "Weird Al" Yankovic Anthology | $17.95 |
| 02502217 | Trisha Yearwood – A Collection of Hits | $16.95 |
| 02500334 | Maury Yeston – December Songs | $17.95 |
| 02502225 | The Maury Yeston Songbook | $19.95 |

See your local music dealer or contact:

**CHERRY LANE MUSIC COMPANY**
6 East 32nd Street, New York, NY 10016

*Quality in Printed Music*

EXCLUSIVELY DISTRIBUTED BY
**HAL•LEONARD CORPORATION**
7777 W. BLUEMOUND RD. P.O. BOX 13819 MILWAUKEE, WI 53213

Prices, contents and availability subject to change without notice.

0404